A CLOSER LOOK
SAINTS

Erika Langmuir

NATIONAL GALLERY COMPANY, LONDON
DISTRIBUTED BY YALE UNIVERSITY PRESS

Erika Langmuir, OBE, was educated in France and the United States. She has taught at the University of Sussex and held the Chair of Art History at the Open University. She was Head of Education at the National Gallery (1988–1995). Erika is author of *Masterpieces* and *The National Gallery Companion Guide*.

Take *A Closer Look* with these guides, produced by the National Gallery, London:
Colour
Conservation
Faces

Front cover: Fra Angelico, *The Virgin Mary with the Apostles and Other Saints*, from the inner left predella panel of the San Domenico Altarpiece, about 1423–4, detail.
Title page: Fra Filippo Lippi, *Seven Saints*, about 1450–3, detail.
Contents page: Rogier van der Weyden, *The Magdalen Reading*, before 1438, detail.

First published in Great Britain as *Pocket Guides: Saints* in 2001
This redesigned edition published 2009
by National Gallery Company Limited
St Vincent House, 30 Orange Street, London WC2H 7HH
ISBN 978 1 85709 465 7
525553
British Library Cataloguing-in-Publication Data
A catalogue record is available from the British Library
Library of Congress Catalog Card Number: 2009932121

PROJECT EDITORS Jan Green (2001 edition) and Giselle Osborne (2009 edition)
EDITOR Jan Green
DESIGN Heather Bowen
COVER ARTWORK Smith & Gilmour
PRODUCTION Jane Hyne and Penny Le Tissier
Printed and bound in Hong Kong by Printing Express

CONTENTS

INTRODUCTION

Recognising Saints

If you enjoy looking at pictures, you may also have, as I do, a soft spot for paintings of saints – whether or not you believe in the saints' special status, their power to intercede with God on our behalf. To walk for the first time into an art gallery or a church, and recognise Saint Catherine of Alexandria with her wheel [2] or Saint Francis of Assisi in his patched friar's tunic [1] is as comforting as running into old friends. And finding them alongside unfamiliar figures like Bishop Emidius, patron saint of Ascoli Piceno in the Italian Marches [3], is like going to the best kind of party, where you know many people but also have the chance to meet new ones.

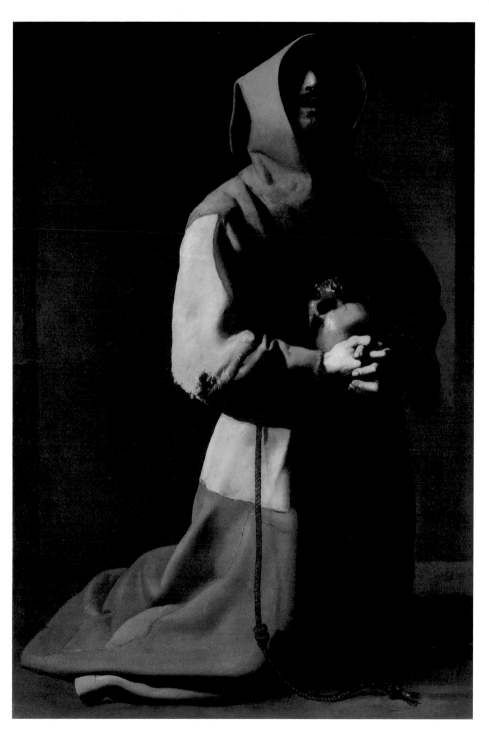

Left: 1. Francisco de Zurbarán, *Saint Francis in Meditation*, 1635–9. This Spanish master worked in the early seventeenth century. His use of strong contrast of light and shadow recalls the work of Caravaggio, and adds drama to his religious paintings.

Right: 2. Raphael, *Saint Catherine of Alexandria*, about 1507. One of the great masters of High Renaissance art, Raphael worked in Urbino and Florence before settling in Rome. He is known for his devotional paintings, portraits, frescos and architecture.

Previous pages: Raphael, *Saint Catherine of Alexandria*, about 1507, detail.

The purpose of this book is not, however, to introduce all, or even most, of the saints. They are listed in many dictionaries, and their stories can be found in anthologies of saints' lives. The most popular of these, and the one most often relied upon by artists, was *The Golden Legend*, written around 1266 by Jacobus de Voragine, Dominican friar and Archbishop of Genoa.

The aim of this book is rather to give a short account of how and why the imagery of saints evolved: who commissioned pictures of saints, how and by whom they might have been viewed, and how they might have influenced attitudes to images in general. Such a small book on such a large subject must by definition be sketchy, and some of it is inevitably speculative and subjective. But one of the great pleasures of old master paintings is that they have gathered centuries of viewing; when we look attentively enough, our gaze mingles with the gazes of long-dead viewers. Although strict historical reconstruction is impossible,

Below: 3. Carlo Crivelli, *The Annunciation, with Saint Emidius*, 1486, detail.

Opposite page: 4. Hans Memling, *The Virgin and Child with Saints and Donors (The Donne Triptych)*, about 1478, detail.

I would like to share with you that sense of empathy with the past that I particularly cherish when looking at pictures of saints – probably the most looked-at images in European history. Since Christian saints are meant to be honoured throughout the Catholic Church, their images have always needed to be universally recognisable, which is why they became so standardised. While there may be little scope for originality in the way saints are represented, there is often room for pictorial wit, a gentle teasing of the viewer. In Hans Memling's *Donne Triptych* [4], the female saint on the extreme left holds the sword with which, according to legend, she was beheaded. As many holy women were killed in this way, it is only when we find the mill wheel in the distance that we can identify her as Saint Catherine. But who are the saints, and why are they shown with objects like the wheel and the sword, which serve as their attributes, or pictorial identity tags?

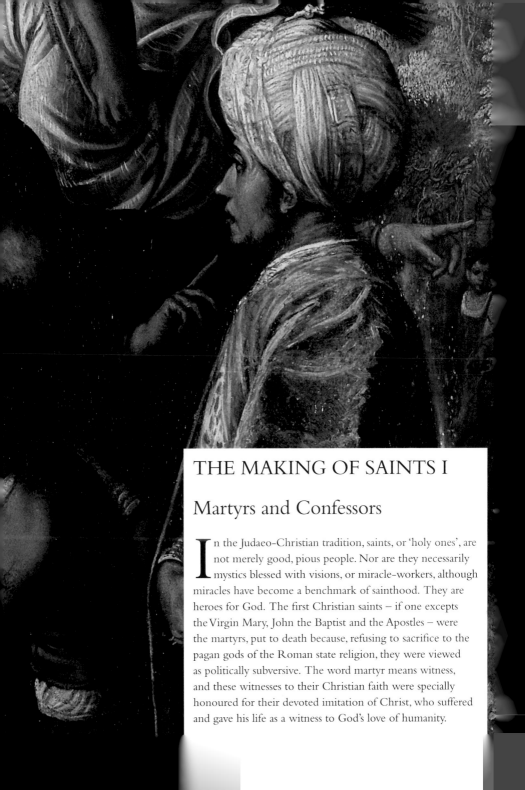

THE MAKING OF SAINTS I

Martyrs and Confessors

In the Judaeo-Christian tradition, saints, or 'holy ones', are not merely good, pious people. Nor are they necessarily mystics blessed with visions, or miracle-workers, although miracles have become a benchmark of sainthood. They are heroes for God. The first Christian saints – if one excepts the Virgin Mary, John the Baptist and the Apostles – were the martyrs, put to death because, refusing to sacrifice to the pagan gods of the Roman state religion, they were viewed as politically subversive. The word martyr means witness, and these witnesses to their Christian faith were specially honoured for their devoted imitation of Christ, who suffered and gave his life as a witness to God's love of humanity.

The earliest record of the cult of a martyr is a letter from the Christians of Smyrna describing the martyrdom of their bishop Polycarp in around the year 156 AD. After his body had been burnt, they collected his bones, 'more precious than jewels', and buried them in a safe place where, 'with the Lord's grace', they could assemble 'to celebrate joyfully the feast-day of his martyrdom'. The celebration would have been joyful because a martyr's death marked victory over death itself: the assurance of immortality in Heaven, in close proximity to God's throne.

Just as the pagans awarded palm branches to victorious athletes, so Christian imagery often awards palms to martyrs. In Adam Elsheimer's *Saint Lawrence prepared for Martyrdom* [5], one of God's angelic messengers, visible only to Lawrence, swoops down from the skies to present the young martyr with his palm. To demonstrate that they are 'unbelievers', Lawrence's persecutors are shown wearing exotic clothes. Their commander is dressed like a Turk, while the costume of the man on the left recalls that of a sixteenth-century German, and may be meant to suggest a Lutheran Protestant. In a final bid to save Lawrence's life, a bearded old man, hooded in black like a Roman priest, urges the saint to worship a stone idol. The ruins in the background are those of ancient Rome. According to legend, Lawrence, a young archdeacon of the Church, was martyred in Rome around the year 258 AD by being roasted on a gridiron – shown in the middle distance with half-naked executioners stoking the raging fire beneath it.

If we know Saint Lawrence's story from having either heard it told or read it in *The Golden Legend*, we can easily grasp the subject of Elsheimer's narrative picture. Nor should we have much difficulty recognising the image of Saint Lawrence in other contexts. The Netherlandish painter Memling [6] represents him without his martyr's palm, giving him a book instead; yet who else but Lawrence could be depicted as a youth in the liturgical dress of a deacon, holding a gridiron? These same attributes help us to recognise him as the saint chatting to Saint Francis in a picture by the Italian friar, Filippo Lippi [7].

Catherine of Alexandria was another third-century martyr, and, like Lawrence's gridiron, her wheel and sword recall the means of her martyrdom. She was, it is said, ordered to be torn to death between spiked wheels. When a burst of fire from Heaven destroyed the wheels, she was decapitated with a sword instead. Even those totally ignorant of her story commemorate both martyr and miracle in the name of a firework, the 'catherine wheel' – and a wheel is the clearest pictorial sign by which we identify her image.

13

Right: 6. Hans Memling, *Saints John the Baptist and Lawrence*, about 1480, detail. Memling was a prolific painter from Bruges. He is an important figure in the Northern Renaissance, an expert with oil paints, and is known for his graceful devotional portraits and religious paintings.

Opposite page: 7. Detail of Fra Filippo Lippi, *Seven Saints*, about 1450–3, showing Saints Francis and Lawrence.

8. Parmigianino, *The Mystic Marriage of Saint Catherine*, about 1527–31. Originally from Parma, as his name suggests, this artist was one of the leading exponents of Mannerism, an elegant, artificial and courtly style of painting that grew from the High Renaissance.

Catherine's legend also recounts a vivid dream she had when she was baptised into the Christian faith. In this dream, the Christ Child on his mother's lap took Catherine to be his celestial bride, slipping a ring on her finger as a token of their mystic marriage. Even though this event long preceded Catherine's martyrdom, Parmigianino includes the spiked wheel in the foreground of his *Mystic Marriage of Saint Catherine* [8]. Indeed, it would seem that the arc and spokes of Saint Catherine's attribute inspired the entire composition: from the round window – whose vertical glazing bar implicitly bisects the whole painting, focusing our gaze on where Christ's and Catherine's hands meet – through the graceful two- and three-dimensional curves in which the figures are posed and the drapery falls.

As we can infer from the letter about the cult of Bishop Polycarp, sanctification of early Christian martyrs was a spontaneous reaction of the Christian communities in which they had lived. Martyrs' feast-days would have been celebrated near their tombs with a communal meal in commemoration of the Lord's Supper. After 313 AD, when Christian worship was legalised throughout the Roman Empire, these meals became the church service of Holy Communion. The martyrs' precious remains were reburied under, or in, the altars at which communion was administered:

> The glorious victims take their place where Christ offers himself as a victim. He who was put to death for all is on the altar; those who have been redeemed by his suffering are under the altar.

These words were written by a fourth-century bishop, Ambrose of Milan, who was himself later declared to be a saint. By this time, bishops had taken it upon themselves to verify the credentials, and sanction the veneration, of martyrs. The precaution was justified: a congregation near Tours had been found worshipping at an altar beneath which were buried the bones ... not of a witness for Christ, but of an executed brigand.

This misplaced zeal was discovered by another fourth-century bishop, Martin of Tours, now better known as Saint Martin. He belongs to another early category of saint: the 'confessor'. Confessor saints are not those who hear the confessions of others, but those who confess – that is, bear public witness to – their faith. They endure heroic hardships and perils, sometimes through persecution, at other times through ascetic practices, but are not actually put to death.

It was obviously harder for artists to assign a pictorial attribute to a confessor than to a martyr – but Saint Martin's early history suggested an unambiguous identifying emblem. He was a soldier before he became a priest. One cold winter day, he rode by a beggar who was dressed only in rags and suffering from the bitter weather. Martin took out his sword, cut his warm cavalry cloak in two, and gave half of it to the beggar. That night he dreamt that Christ appeared to him, saying: 'What you have done for that poor man, you have done unto me.'

It was not this somewhat tepid good deed which earned Martin sainthood, but rather the total of his life in the service of Christ. Yet because the story is unique to him, he is usually depicted on horseback, cutting his cloak in half, with a small ragged beggar in tow. But this is not how he appears in a fragment of the altarpiece commissioned by Bernardinus de Salviatis for the Collegiate Church of St Donatian in Bruges [9].

Bernardinus, a canon of the church, had himself portrayed kneeling at prayer, looking towards the cross on the altarpiece's right-hand panel (probably a Crucifixion now in Berlin). He wears the vestments of his office: a black cassock edged with brown fur, and over it a pleated white tunic, the rochet. On his left arm he carries an almuce, or hooded cape, of grey fur. Bernardinus is being presented to Christ by his name saint – the saint whose name he was given at baptism – the Franciscan preacher Bernardino of Siena (1380–1444). On the right stands the titular saint of the church and patron saint of Bruges, Donatian, a fourth-century bishop and martyr. Dressed in archbishop's vestments contemporary with the painting, Donatian holds his emblem of a wheel set with five candles. According to legend, such a wheel was floated down the river into which he had been thrown. It stopped over the spot where his drowned body lay, and he was recovered and brought back to life by prayer.

It would have been unseemly, in this solemn ecclesiastical company, to introduce Saint Martin as a soldier – nor would the format of the panel have allowed him to appear mounted on his horse next to the other figures.

Gerard David therefore depicts Martin as a bishop, but gives us two clues to his identity. The very sharp-eyed viewer might just make out that his morse – the jewelled clasp of his red velvet cope – is set with a scene of a man cutting his cloak in half to give to a crouching beggar. For those of us with merely normal eyesight, David has painted a beggar in the landscape behind the holy bishop – a beggar in whom we recognise the saint's attribute, just as we recognise Saint Catherine's wheel in the mill wheel in the background of Memling's *Donne Triptych* [4].

9. Gerard David, *Canon Bernardijn Salviati and Three Saints*, after 1501. This Northern Renaissance painter came to prominence in Bruges in the early sixteenth century. His paintings borrow heavily from earlier Belgian masters and his ability to paint textures was widely admired.

THE CULT OF SAINTS

Relics and Images

Early Christians, gathered around the tombs of local martyrs and confessors, venerated these witnesses to the faith through their relics – the saints' physical remains or objects they had touched – not their images. They would have been amazed at the paintings reproduced here. Relics came to be regarded as offering protection against misfortune or ill-health, or as agents of healing; some appeared to be more efficacious than others. Once saints' relics were 'translated', that is, removed from tombs to altars, they could be divided, split into fragments – increasingly so as churches and altars proliferated. Competition between churches and shrines, and a brisk trade in relics, ensued, because effective relics attracted both pilgrims and trade. As local cults of martyrs and confessors spread further afield, means had to be found of identifying which saint was connected with which altar. Images of saints might be said to have originated as illustrated labels, indicating the titular saint in whose memory Christ's sacrifice was re-enacted at a particular altar. In due course, these images became banners to which people rallied, defining their own identity and allegiances through their choice of patron saints, whose pictures they carried in processions.

Left: 10. Lucas Cranach the Elder, *Saints Genevieve and Apollonia*, 1506, detail. One of the most prominent artists of the German Renaissance, Cranach was a prolific painter of portraits, and religious and mythological scenes. He knew Martin Luther and had ties to the Protestant Reformation.

Above: 11. Master of Liesborn, *Saints Cosmas and Damian and the Virgin*, probably 1470–80.

Previous pages: Follower of Quinten Massys, *Saint Luke painting the Virgin and Child*, about 1520?, detail.

By the second millennium, European society was recovering from the barbarian invasions and civil wars that had destroyed the Roman Empire. Monastic orders had cleared new tracts of countryside for agriculture. Cities were founded or expanding, and within them associations of artisans and merchants were formed. Dioceses – districts under the jurisdiction of a bishop – were subdivided into parishes. Parishes spawned benevolent confraternities, whose members were joined in devotional practices and good works. Early Christian communities had sheltered around their martyrs and confessors, and individuals were placed under the protection of saints in whose name they were baptised. Each of these new institutions required its own saintly advocate and to this end, centuries-old local cults were promoted or revived. Cities often chose as their patron their first martyred bishop, like Saint Emidius who holds a model of Ascoli Piceno [3], or Bruges' Saint Donatian [9]. Paris gallantly adopted Saint Genevieve, the fifth-century heroine of a siege by barbarian Franks and Huns [10]. The fourth-century doctor-martyrs, Saints Cosmas and Damian, became the patrons of doctors and hospitals [11], while painters venerated Saint Luke,

Left: 12. Follower of Quinten Massys, *Saint Luke painting the Virgin and Child*, about 1520? Massys worked primarily in Antwerp during the early sixteenth century. He painted devotional images but perhaps is now best remembered for his caricatures, which were enormously popular and widely copied.

Above: Detail of *Saint Bernard's Vision of the Virgin.*

Opposite page: 13. Fra Filippo Lippi, *Saint Bernard's Vision of the Virgin,* 1447.

evangelist, physician and legendary portraitist of the Virgin Mary
[12]. But new institutions also felt the need for new saints. Monastic orders naturally put forward their own founders, like the
Cistercians' Saint Bernard of Clairvaux [13], or the Benedictines'
Saint Benedict and his sister Saint Scholastica, shown here with
Saint John the Evangelist [14]. As more religious orders were
created, their founders too would be candidates for sanctification.
Mystics and visionaries, charitable royals, ascetic nuns, charismatic
preachers, all had their devotees. By the fifteenth century, when
portraiture from life had become commonplace and casts were
made of the faces of the illustrious dead, images of newly made
saints became recognisable not only through their attributes but
also through their likeness.

Bernardino of Siena, declared a saint shortly after his death in
1444, had been famous for promoting the adoration of the name
of Jesus, in the form of the Greek monogram IHS, transcribed
into Latin as Iesus Hominum Salvator, Jesus Saviour of Mankind.

Above: 14. Master of Liesborn,
*Saints John the Evangelist,
Scholastica and Benedict*, probably
1470–80.

Opposite page: 15. Gerard David
*Canon Bernardijn Salviati and
Three Saints*, after 1501, detail.

Following pages, left: 16. Moretto
da Brescia, *The Virgin and Child
with Saint Bernardino and Other
Saints*, about 1540–5. This late
Renaissance artist worked in
Brescia, Northern Italy, and Venice.
His many portraits and large
altarpieces are heavily influenced
by the Venetian master, Titian.

Following pages, right: 17. Guercino,
*Saint Gregory the Great with Saints
Ignatius Loyola and Francis Xavier*,
about 1625–6. This self-taught artist
absorbed the influences of early
Baroque masters Caravaggio and
the Carracci family.

This monogram, along with his grey Franciscan habit and his friar's tonsure, became Bernardino's attribute. The Netherlandish painter, Gerard David, relies on it to identify the saint in Canon Bernardinus's altarpiece [15]. The better-informed Italian Moretto, however, also gives Bernardino sunken cheeks and grey hair, approximating the preacher's appearance at the time of his death [16]. The National Gallery does not house any closer likeness of the saint, but any traveller in Bernardino's native Tuscany will instantly recognise the old man's toothless face in countless pictures based on his death mask moulded in plaster.

In the same way, Lombardy is chock-a-block with images of the sixteenth-century archbishop of Milan, Charles Borromeo, declared a saint in 1610, and identifiable by his prominent aquiline nose and five-o'clock shadow. Charles's friend and adviser, the white-haired and bearded Philip Neri, founder of the Oratorians and declared saint in 1622, is equally recognisable, as are the Jesuit saints Ignatius Loyola (left) and Francis Xavier, shown here on either side of Saint Gregory the Great [17]. Portrait-based images like these not only aid identification, but also foster that sense of friendly intimacy with the saints as real and familiar people.

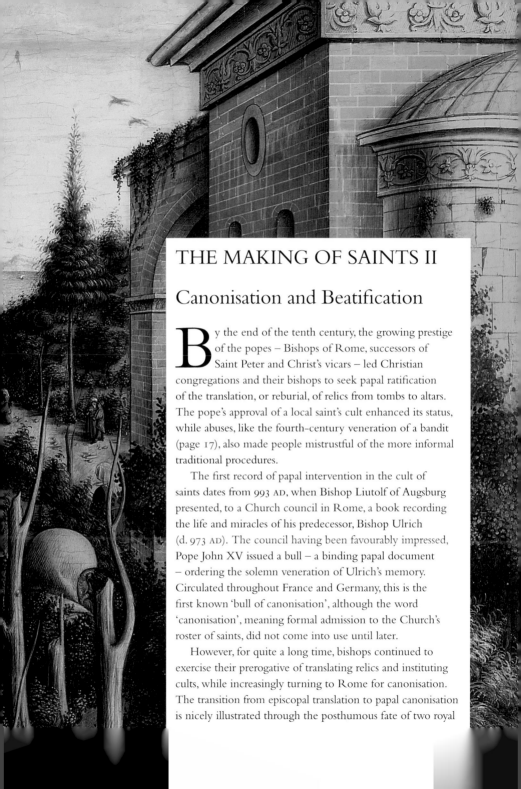

THE MAKING OF SAINTS II

Canonisation and Beatification

By the end of the tenth century, the growing prestige of the popes – Bishops of Rome, successors of Saint Peter and Christ's vicars – led Christian congregations and their bishops to seek papal ratification of the translation, or reburial, of relics from tombs to altars. The pope's approval of a local saint's cult enhanced its status, while abuses, like the fourth-century veneration of a bandit (page 17), also made people mistrustful of the more informal traditional procedures.

The first record of papal intervention in the cult of saints dates from 993 AD, when Bishop Liutolf of Augsburg presented, to a Church council in Rome, a book recording the life and miracles of his predecessor, Bishop Ulrich (d. 973 AD). The council having been favourably impressed, Pope John XV issued a bull – a binding papal document – ordering the solemn veneration of Ulrich's memory. Circulated throughout France and Germany, this is the first known 'bull of canonisation', although the word 'canonisation', meaning formal admission to the Church's roster of saints, did not come into use until later.

However, for quite a long time, bishops continued to exercise their prerogative of translating relics and instituting cults, while increasingly turning to Rome for canonisation. The transition from episcopal translation to papal canonisation is nicely illustrated through the posthumous fate of two royal

English saints [18]. Edmund, last king of East Anglia, was in
870 AD killed with arrows by invading Danes for refusing
to abjure his Christian faith. Having become the object of
veneration, his remains were moved around 915 AD to the church
of the Benedictine abbey which later became known as Bury
St. Edmunds. Edward the Confessor, last Anglo-Saxon king, died
in 1066, having promised the succession to his cousin William
of Normandy. His canonisation in 1161 by Pope Alexander
III may have had as much to do with Alexander's gratitude
for William's support against the German Emperor, Frederic
Barbarossa, as with Edward's own monkish virtues.

Gradually, the balance of power in the making of saints
shifted in favour of papal authority. In 1234, during the papacy of
Gregory IX, the exclusive right of popes to canonise was inscribed
in the laws of the Roman Church. Papal commissions were
appointed to investigate the life and miracles of candidates, and
legal requirements for sanctity were established. The examination
resembled – and continues to resemble – a legal trial, with
advocates, sworn witnesses and a prosecuting counsel, popularly
known as the Devil's Advocate, charged with opposing attempts at
canonisation by all lawful means. In theory, the papacy also reserved
for itself the right to approve local cults, observed within a single
diocese. Such 'beatification', from the Latin word for 'blessing',
has become a normal prerequisite for canonisation, although
canonisation is not an inevitable consequence of beatification.

In practice, local cults, such as that of Saint Edmund, continued
to flourish and even to multiply without papal consent. The
words 'blessed' and 'saint' were for a long while applied without
distinction to all those who were venerated, whether canonised
or not. Despite protests by some, images continued to be erected
to both. Indeed, images, because they attracted the devout to
altars and shrines, came to be used as arguments for canonisation.
Artists tended to endow both the blessed and saints with haloes –
a zone of light around the head that had from time immemorial
been the visual attribute of gods and saints. By the second half of
the fourteenth century, however, a firmer distinction had been
made. Circular haloes were reserved for saints, while the blessed
were to be adorned merely with rays of light [19].

Nonetheless, the rapid increase of new cults led to fears that
the true faith was being diluted. The Florentine writer Franco
Sacchetti (1330–1400) complained in a letter to a friend that
the various religious orders, greedy for alms and offerings, were
erecting so many altars to celebrate 'new saints' that belief in the
'old ones' was undermined:

19. Carlo Crivelli, *The Vision of the Blessed Gabriele*, probably about 1489. Born in Venice, Crivelli settled in north-east Italy. He is a Renaissance artist with an interest in depicting the natural world.

Who can assure that there are not many who suspect that the old saints began in the same way; the rays around their head and the inscription 'blessed' at their feet may in time have been converted, the rays into haloes, and the blessed into a saint? How can we believe in these our priests, who elevate the body of these Blessed so high, and there put candles and images; while Our Lord and the Virgin Mary are painted low, near the floor and in the dark without any light? ... And not long ago I saw in a row of five paintings three Saints and two Blessed ... and the Pope does not attend to it, he has better things to do.

20. Paolo Uccello, *Saint George and the Dragon*, about 1470. Uccello worked in Florence in the fifteenth century. He pioneered the application of perspective theory to convey realistic space and depth in his paintings.

Sacchetti's scruples resemble those of sixteenth-century Protestant Reformers, who saw the veneration of saints as detracting from the worship of Christ. Today, even relatively recently some Roman Catholics are perturbed by the late Pope John Paul II's unprecedented partiality for canonisation, and disapproved of his choice of new saints. Throughout the history of the Western Church, the making and unmaking of saints has always been a controversial matter, revealing tensions and conflicts between local interests and central power; between religious orders and regular clergy; between clergy and laity; scholarship and popular piety. Many patriotic Englishmen and women – by no means all Roman Catholics, or even believing Christians – were distressed when a recent papal reform removed Saint George, patron of England, from the Roman Calendar, demoting him from martyr to pious legend. But if he is no longer venerated at Catholic altars, his image survives, encouraging us to fight the good fight, and vanquish evil's dragon [20]. It is his image, and not his cult, that has made Saint George famous, a glamorous emblem and role model of chivalrous courage and faith.

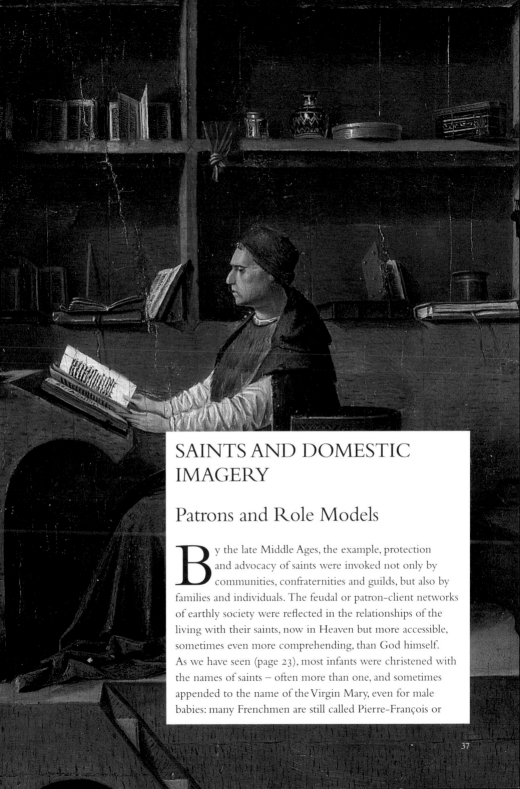

SAINTS AND DOMESTIC IMAGERY

Patrons and Role Models

By the late Middle Ages, the example, protection and advocacy of saints were invoked not only by communities, confraternities and guilds, but also by families and individuals. The feudal or patron-client networks of earthly society were reflected in the relationships of the living with their saints, now in Heaven but more accessible, sometimes even more comprehending, than God himself. As we have seen (page 23), most infants were christened with the names of saints – often more than one, and sometimes appended to the name of the Virgin Mary, even for male babies: many Frenchmen are still called Pierre-François or

Jean-Marie. People's 'name days', the days of their name saints in the liturgical calendar, were celebrated more readily than their birthdays. This was not merely because saints' days, normally the anniversaries of their death, were publicly observed and therefore more easily remembered: it was also a mark of Christian faith. As an early fifteenth-century cleric wrote in a sermon honouring Saint Jerome on his feast-day of 30 September:

> For if blind antiquity was accustomed to celebrate the birthday of human beings, the day on which they were conducted into this miserable life where needs of every sort abound, how much the more should we who are illumined by true faith treasure the feast-day of God's saints, the day on which they are conveyed into a life free from death, safe from catastrophe, and immune from all adversity!

The bond with one's own name saint was naturally more intimate than that with other saints; in addition to 'Christian name' saints, special allegiances to saints were forged through family names.

All this was naturally reflected in the production of images. By the fifteenth century, most Christian homes in Europe would have had at least one picture of a particularly revered saint, from a cheap woodcut bought at a fair to specially commissioned works by leading artists – like Filippo Lippi's *Seven Saints*, probably dating from the mid-1450s [21]. The shape of this panel, once part of the furnishings of the Palazzo Medici in Florence, suggests that it may have been set over a door. The picture is thought to have been commissioned from the Medici's favoured painter by either Piero di Cosimo de'Medici (1414–69) or his cousin, Pierfrancesco di Lorenzo di Giovanni di Bicci de'Medici (1430–77). (Like the Anglo-French prefix 'Fitz', 'di ...' means 'son of ...'.) All these forenames are names of saints, each of whom appears here. Filippo was given the challenging task of designing a coherent composition of seven male figures, associated only through their names' importance to the Medici dynasty.

His solution may have been inspired by the kind of Renaissance altarpiece often referred to as a 'sacra conversazione',

22. Fra Filippo Lippi, *The Annunciation*, about 1450–3.

in which the Virgin Mary, enthroned with the Christ Child, is surrounded by saints, all seemingly communing together. Here, in the absence of the Virgin Mary, the earliest and most important of the Medici name saints, Giovanni Battista, John the Baptist, also a patron saint of Florence, sits in the centre of a stone bench that accommodates all the figures and subtly echoes the shape of the panel. Pointing upwards, he bears witness to the key event of his life, when he perceived the Holy Spirit descending upon Jesus at the Baptism: 'And I saw, and bare record that this is the Son of God' (John 1:34). He is flanked by two saints in doctors' robes and caps; one looks up to heaven in wonder, the other prays. These are the brothers Cosmas and Damian, the charitable early Christian doctors and martyrs, patrons of the family whose name, Medici, means physicians in Italian. Beside them sit Saint

Lawrence (Lorenzo), with his gridiron, and the elderly hermit Saint Anthony Abbot (Antonio). Lawrence's hands are folded in prayer, but his eyes are fixed on the radiant wounds in the hands of Saint Francis (Francesco), miraculously replicating those of the crucified Christ. Anthony, echoing the Baptist, turns to Peter (Piero) – not the apostle Saint Peter but the Dominican preacher named after him, Saint Peter Martyr, who listens meditatively. His attribute, a cleaver permanently fixed in his head, refers to his own martyrdom at the hands of heretics.

Filippo has related these figures to each other visually, and, more importantly, psychologically; and he has related them in a quite particular way to the original viewer or viewers. These male saints inhabit a world somewhere between Heaven and Florence. Like any respectable Florentine citizens – that is, men and property owners – of a certain age and gravity, they meet on a garden bench to discuss matters of common interest. But their conversation is not of politics, or business, or errant children and grandchildren. They address questions of eternal and universal import: Christ's divinity; bearing witness for one's faith; the need for charity, for meditation and prayer. Images of saints in the home not only provide a focus for devotion; they are there to remind viewers daily of the spiritual dimension of their lives.

Yet saints could also be enlisted as role models to enforce secular social ideals. In the companion panel of *The Annunciation*, also by Filippo Lippi and possibly intended for the room of a female member of the family [22], the Virgin Mary submits to God's will: 'Behold the handmaid of the Lord; be it unto me according to thy word' (Luke 1:38). Holiest of the saints, Mary has been sitting alone in her bedroom, reading a prayer book. The Archangel Gabriel's appearance, in the enclosed garden which symbolises Mary's virginity, also signifies the moment of the miraculous conception of her Child. A scattering of gold rays emanates from her womb to meet the dove of the Holy Spirit launched from the top of the panel. The male Medici name saints John, Cosmas and Damian, Lawrence, Anthony, Francis and Peter Martyr are pictured in company, conversing. Filippo's image of Mary reflects the other side of the coin: the Florentine Renaissance ideal of a retiring, chaste, devout, submissive but fertile wife.

Piety and Art

Filippo's panels are beautifully painted and highly decorative, but I think we can assume that, to their Medici owners, their value as works of art was secondary to their social and religious functions. This need not have been true of all domestic images of saints.

Jerome (?347–420 AD), monk and translator of the standard Latin version of the Bible, the Vulgate, became in the fifteenth century a favourite subject of small pictures for the home. We cannot always tell how, or by whom, these paintings were meant to be viewed (not all the people who commissioned them can have been called Jerome). The question is complicated by the fact that images of Jerome tend to fall into one of two categories. The saint is shown either in penitence in the wilderness, as in Dürer's wonderful little panel of around 1496 [23], or as a scholar snugly installed in his study, as in Antonello da Messina's equally magical, and only slightly larger, work of some twenty years earlier [24].

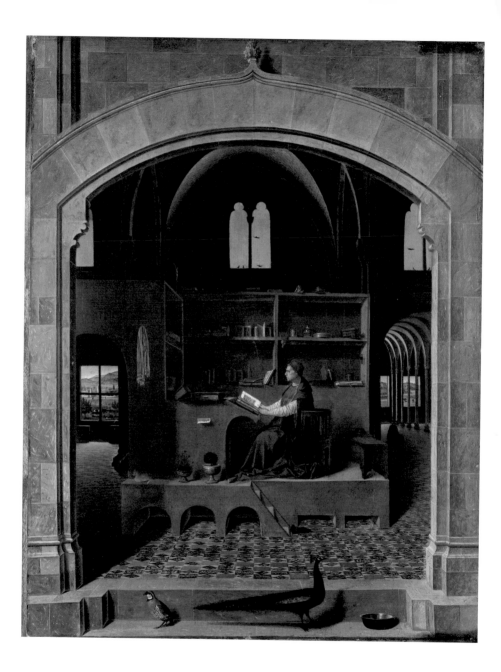

24. Antonello da Messina, *Saint Jerome in his Study*, about 1475. This Renaissance artist hailed from Sicily. He shows various Northern Renaissance influences (although it is unlikely he travelled there), such as the skilful use of oil paint to achieve extraordinary detail in his paintings.

Both types of image are based on biographical fact and tradition. The office of cardinal did not exist in Jerome's lifetime, but as a papal adviser he is normally given a cardinal's red hat and cloak. Legend attributed to him another saint's good deed, extracting a thorn from a lion's foot, and he is normally pictured with a tame lion. Both types – Jerome as penitent and Jerome as scholar – originated as exhortations to the spiritual life, but their definitions of this differ. In the penitent version, Jerome beats his breast with a stone while contemplating a crucifix. Dürer shows him holding a book, which can only be the Bible. But a contemporary viewer would have known that before he turned to collating and translating Scripture, Jerome retired to the Syrian desert repenting of his earlier devotion to pagan writers. This category of image – if not Dürer's particular one – deprecates intellectual achievement in favour of direct empathy with Christ, and the emulation of his sufferings through penitential practices. It is a view of Jerome, supposed founder of western monasticism, made popular in the newly formed, ascetic Hieronymite convents (Hieronymus is the Latin form of Jerome). Antonello's alternative, conversely, celebrates book learning, the transmission of the Word of God through written texts. While both versions elevate contemplation above action, they are diametrically opposed in their ideal of how the contemplative life should be lived.

Must we then suppose that Dürer's patron (or, if the painting was made for sale on the open market, the picture's buyer) was an anti-intellectual devoted to a life of penance, and that Antonello's was a studious theologian, claiming Jerome as patron of his academic endeavours?

The latter appears more probable, and a modern art historian has indeed suggested that Antonello has here portrayed a learned cardinal in the guise of Saint Jerome. The picture is, however, first recorded only in 1529, when it belonged to a non-clerical Venetian art lover. And a closer comparison of both paintings suggests that they may always have been intended rather more as works of art than as objects of piety.

Dürer's Jerome [23] is a noble figure, but a stereotypical one: the freshest and most affecting passages of the picture are the descriptions of nature, from the vivid finches in the foreground, through the wooded crags to the snow-capped mountains on the horizon, the rising or setting sun warring against clouds. The pitched roof of a Gothic castle rises above oaks and firs; the lacy tracery of a dead tree is silhouetted against the sky. Dürer's 'Syrian desert' is alive with vegetation, and the saint and his lion rest by the rippling waters of a swiftly running stream. Jerome's

Right and opposite: Albrecht Dürer,
Saint Jerome, about 1496, details
showing a finch and a dead tree
silhouetted against the sky.

crucifix is wedged in the stump of a silver birch tree. Whatever
their burden of religious symbolism, these details draw the eye
through their exact and poetic evocation of the visible world,
as Dürer had experienced it on his momentous voyages across
the Alps. Holding this tiny picture in the hand and gazing into
its depths as in a crystal ball, its owner could undertake a journey
of the imagination, sharing the artist's wonder and delight in the
capacity of art to recreate the plenitude of God's creation.

Antonello's impassive and immobile Saint Jerome [24],
absorbed in his book, is more remote from the viewer than
Dürer's. Not content with recreating remembered experience,
the painter has imagined a fantastical interior, part-church, part-
palace, part-library. But this artificial setting is animated by what
appears to be real light moving through real space and casting real
shadows. One light source originates in the viewer's own space
in front of the picture – as if our gaze, entering through the large
opening in the stone façade, itself illuminated the scene within.
But sunlight also streams in through windows deep within the
painting; beyond them the sky is alive with birds, there are fields
and mountains, a minuscule walled city, a river, people boating or
fishing – vistas receding to the horizon and seeming to continue
beyond. Even more than Dürer, Antonello demands the viewer's
active collaboration: the harder we look, the more we see. In an

age before photography, when even mirrors were scarce, this level of representational skill would have seemed little short of miraculous.

Both these works evoke religious sentiments, but they are above all – and surely always were – a source of aesthetic pleasure. The growing demand for domestic images of saints ultimately led the affluent classes to value the craft of painting itself, especially for its ability to represent in two dimensions the appearance of a three-dimensional world. Where an earlier generation of the wealthy had amassed objects in rare and costly materials, by the late fifteenth century their descendants had learned to prize artistic skill above material value, and had begun to collect pictures by the best and most innovative painters.

The conflation of piety with visual enjoyment was not confined to the rich and sophisticated, as an anecdote in Vasari's *Life of Michelangelo* suggests. Vasari records the great artist's affection for a rustic itinerant painter who made crude little pictures of saints to sell to Tuscan country people. One of this man's anecdotes which most amused Michelangelo concerned a peasant who had ordered an image of Saint Francis of Assisi. He was dismayed that the saint's habit, adopted by Francis as a symbol of humility and poverty, was so dull and sad in colour. To please him, the painter gave Francis a richly decorated priest's vestment, although the saintly friar had only been a deacon and was never ordained, and the peasant went away happy with his picture. Similar considerations may have prompted Botticelli to set the drab figure of the saint against a gold-leaf background and surround him with multi-coloured angels [25].

But where precisely, the modern gallery visitor may wish to ask, did piety end and aesthetic appreciation begin? We tend now to believe that the two are distinct, yet in past ages the question may never have arisen. The Tuscan peasant wished both to have a bit of beautiful bright colour on his wall and to honour his favourite saint. An innovative artist wanted to show off his powers, but this does not mean that he treated the subject of his painting cynically. An owner/viewer may sometimes have turned to a saint's image for comfort and edification, and at other times as one would to any picture, for pleasure, but mainly, one suspects, for both reasons simultaneously: spiritual refreshment. Most of us have lost this double viewpoint – perhaps because religion and the saints are no longer part of our daily lives and affections.

Private Viewing and Public Issues

Yet another complicating factor in the private viewing of saints' images is that, just as they could be used to enforce secular ideals [22], so they were also enlisted in contemporary controversies.

For the modern spectator, probably the most difficult picture of Saint Jerome in the Gallery is that painted by Domenichino in about 1602, shortly after his arrival in Rome from his native Bologna [26]. By 1603 it was in the collection of Cardinal Pietro Aldobrandini, nephew of Pope Clement VIII.

Domenichino situates Jerome in a grotto-study in the wilderness, combining the two strands of the saint's imagery. He introduces two, more startling, novelties. The saint appears almost as naked, and every bit as muscular, as Michelangelo's monumental nudes in the Sistine Chapel. Jerome's work of biblical translation appears to be dictated to him by an angel – a detail which is associated with the imagery of the evangelist Saint Matthew, but is not part of the pictorial or biographical tradition of Jerome.

What is going on, and how was this – to us rather disagreeable – picture viewed? Has Domenichino confused Jerome with Matthew, and is he just showing off his newly acquired knowledge of Michelangelo? What was the painting's significance for Cardinal Aldobrandini?

By the end of the sixteenth century, the Vulgate, Jerome's Latin version of the Scriptures, had come under attack. Humanist scholars, better trained in Hebrew, Greek and Aramaic than Jerome, had discovered inaccuracies in his translation. Alternative texts were proposed, claiming greater fidelity to the Word of God. Protestants throughout Europe challenged Rome by producing translations in modern, spoken languages, so that the Bible, hitherto reserved for the clergy alone, could be read by everyone. The authority of the standard text used throughout the Roman Church, and the whole edifice of the Church with it, was undermined.

To defend Jerome and his translation was therefore to defend Catholic tradition, and papal supremacy itself. The Pope, prohibiting scholarly criticism and other translations, reaffirmed the Vulgate's authority. And that, of course, is the prime meaning of Domenichino's picture for the Pope's nephew. Like the prophets of the Old Testament or the evangelists, Saint Jerome is divinely inspired; an angel, God's messenger, instructs him. The saint's nudity is symbolic, recalling – via Michelangelo – the divinities and heroes of pagan myth. Jerome has become a Hercules for Christ, labouring to purge Christendom of dissent and heresy just as Hercules laboured to cleanse the Augean stables.

26. Domenichino, *The Vision of Saint Jerome*, before 1603. Domenichino worked in Rome, Bologna and Naples. He was a pupil of Ludovico Carracci, a member of the successful artistic family. He made primarily religious works in the dramatic Baroque style.

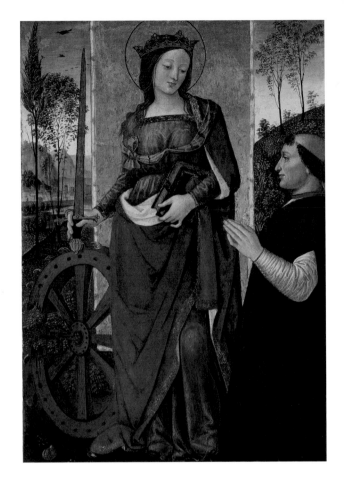

Right: 27. Pintoricchio, *Saint Catherine of Alexandria with a Donor*, probably about 1480–1500 This painter began his career in Perugia and, while working in Rome, had received important commissions from the Papacy, including frescos in the Vatican.

Opposite page: 28. Francesco di Giorgio, *Saint Dorothy and the Infant Christ*, probably 1460s. A successful painter and sculptor in mid-fifteenth century Siena, Francesco eventually turned his career more toward architecture and engineering, and worked for various courts around Italy.

Piety and Gender

Reformers complained that the statues of female saints in churches were too beautiful and too richly dressed, more like courtesans than holy women. In the private sphere the potential for confusion could be even greater. Once again, the modern gallery visitor is at a disadvantage in trying to reconstruct the artists' original intentions and their contemporary viewers' responses. The most popular female saints, such as Saint Catherine of Alexandria, were venerated equally often by women and men, and their imagery reflects this [2, 27].

On the other hand, we can well believe that a charming small picture of Saint Dorothy, probably designed in the 1460s by the Sienese artist, architect and engineer Francesco di Giorgio, was made for the devotions of a woman named Dorothy [28].

Detail of *Saint Dorothy and the Infant Christ.*

In many respects it resembles the somewhat later picture of Saint Francis in fig. 25: the saint is shown against a gold-leaf background. The effect, however, is even more decorative. Dorothy, a Christian virgin martyr put to death around 300 AD, is a graceful young woman, elegantly dressed and carrying a sprig of carnations. As she was being led to execution, legend has it, a pagan lawyer named Theophilus mocked her, asking her to send him flowers and fruit from the garden of Paradise. Miraculously, a heavenly child (here the Christ Child himself) appeared with a basket of apples and roses, which she had sent to Theophilus, who was converted to Christianity as a consequence and was subsequently also martyred.

We are spared the martyrdom and shown the miracle – the saint's identifying attribute – whose secular counterpart, the love and cultivation of flowers, was a suitable female accomplishment. The saint, patron also of brides and newly weds, was in every way an acceptable role model for a young woman, and the painting a welcome embellishment of any woman's chamber.

29. Anthony van Dyck, *Lady Elizabeth Thimbelby and Dorothy, Viscountess Andover*, about 1637. Originally from Antwerp, Van Dyck worked with Rubens, before becoming a successful portrait artist in Italy. In 1632, Van Dyck moved to England, becoming court painter to Charles I, and was widely sought after by the aristocracy for his grand portraits.

Nearly two hundred years later, in 1637, Anthony van Dyck painted the two married daughters of Thomas, Viscount Savage [29]. Elizabeth, standing on the left, had married Sir John Thimbelby, a notable recusant (a Catholic who refused to attend Anglican services) in 1634. In 1637 her sister Dorothy caused public scandal by eloping with the Catholic Charles Howard, Viscount Andover.

The painting is most obviously a double portrait celebrating the friendship of two sisters, on the occasion of the elder's marriage. To most educated English viewers of the period, the winged child may have seemed a Cupid bringing flowers to the bride – but the picture also has another meaning. To Van Dyck and his sitters, all three Catholics in an aggressively Protestant country, the winged child with his basket was the attribute of Saint Dorothy. Like Sebastiano del Piombo in the previous century [30] or Gonzales Coques some fifty years later [31], Van Dyck identifies his sitter through the traditional visual clues to

57

30. Attributed to Sebastiano del Piombo, *Portrait of a Lady with the Attributes of Saint Agatha*, about 1540. Sebastiano was working in Rome during the early sixteenth century. He was a close associate of Michelangelo, whose influence is evident in the types of figures shown in his paintings.

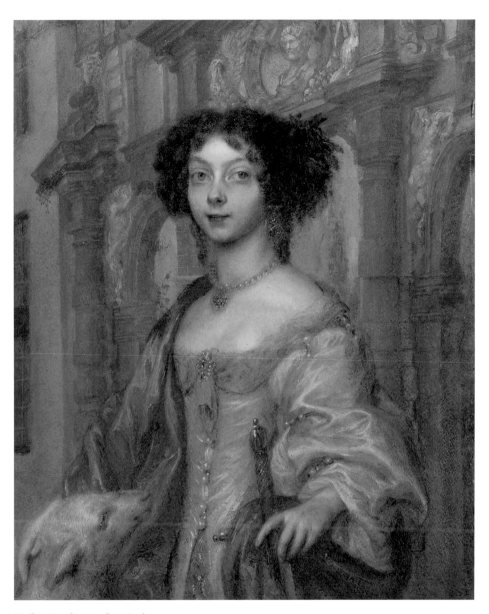

31. Gonzales Coques, *Portrait of a Woman as Saint Agnes*, about 1680. Based in Antwerp during the seventeenth century, his fine portraits won him consistent commissions from the Royal House of Orange and Spanish Royalty, before settling in the Netherlands.

Above: 32. Annibale Carracci,
The Dead Christ Mourned, about
1604. As a member of a famed
family of artists, Annibale Carracci
was one of the pre-eminent
painters of his time, admired for
his richly colourful and dramatic
religious and mythological scenes.

Following pages: Detail of *The
Dead Christ Mourned* showing
Mary Magdalene.

her name (Sebastiano's portrait shows the martyred Saint Agatha's
breasts on a plate in the background, together with the shears
used to cut them off; Gonzales Coques's lady caresses a lamb, in
Latin agnus, punning attribute of Saint Agnes). But in its precise
context Van Dyck's device suggests more. Dorothy, Viscountess
Andover, assumes the identity of Saint Dorothy; invoking the
protection of her very own saint, she may also be declaring her
readiness to suffer martyrdom (or at least social disgrace) for her
love and her faith.

These works by Francesco di Giorgio, Van Dyck, Sebastiano
and Coques in no way exclude male spectators, but all seem to
have been primarily adapted to women viewers and sitters. But
what of the imagery of that most problematic female saint, Mary
Magdalene? Her scandalous past, constructed by male theologians
from various unconnected passages of the Bible, made her a
dubious role model for unmarried girls, wives and mothers. Her
later history, however, singled her out as the supreme Christian

penitent and contemplative. The loving sinner, privileged to be the first to see the risen Christ, became in a sense a counterpart of his loving mother, the Virgin Mary. For many centuries, these two Maries together exemplified a male view of womanhood, at the same time transcending gender to achieve universal relevance. But, unlike the Virgin's, the Magdalen's image may have been, I think, most often intended for the gaze of male spectators.

In the Gospels, Mary of Magdala was one of Jesus' women followers, who ministered to him as he preached in Galilee; he had healed her of demonic possession by seven evil spirits (Luke 8:1-2). She was present at his crucifixion. With two other women, she went to his tomb with spices to anoint his body, and found the tomb empty (Mark 16:1-8). It was to her that the risen Christ first appeared on the morning of Easter Sunday (Mark 16:9; John 20:11-18). The Roman Church traditionally identified this Mary with Martha's sister, Mary of Bethany. After supper in honour of Jesus, who had raised their brother Lazarus from the dead (John 11:18-45), she 'took ... a pound of ointment of spikenard, very costly, and anointed the feet of Jesus, and wiped his feet with her hair' (John 12:3). Mary Magdalene was finally also conflated with the unnamed sinner, a 'woman in the city' who, in the Pharisee's house, also anointed Jesus' feet with her hair, her tears mingling with the costly ointment she brought in an alabaster box. It is of her that Jesus said: 'Her sins, which are many, are forgiven; for she loved much: but to whom little is forgiven, the same loveth little' (Luke 8:37-50).

This composite Mary Magdalene, like all saints, has her place in altarpieces and other church paintings, where she appears most frequently in scenes of Christ's crucifixion and entombment. Images like these could also be painted on a small scale for private viewing and devotion. A particularly beautiful example is Annibale Carracci's *The Dead Christ Mourned* or *'The Three Maries'* of around 1604 [32]. The subject was inspired by medieval meditational texts that introduced a scene of lamentation between the biblical accounts of Christ's death on the cross and his burial. Unusually, Annibale depicts only women mourners, and implies a slightly earlier moment, also often represented in art: the Pietà - the Virgin taking leave of her Son, laid across her lap in death as he had lain in sleep as an infant. Here, Mary faints with grief. She falls back, and Christ's body slides off her lap onto the ground. Two of the women – probably Mary, the mother of James, and Mary Salome, who will return to the tomb on Easter morning with Mary Magdalene (Mark 16:1) – hurry to her aid, distressed on her behalf. The Magdalen herself, younger and

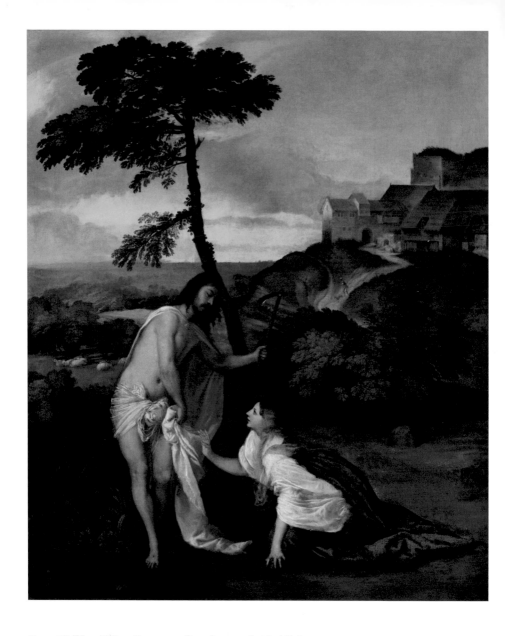

Above: 33. Titian, *Noli me Tangere*, about 1514. Titian is widely regarded as the finest painter of Renaissance Venice. His richly coloured, painterly style and dynamic compositions made Titian one of the most sought-after painters of his day, with his work in demand throughout Europe.

Opposite page: Detail of *Noli me Tangere*, showing Mary Magdalene.

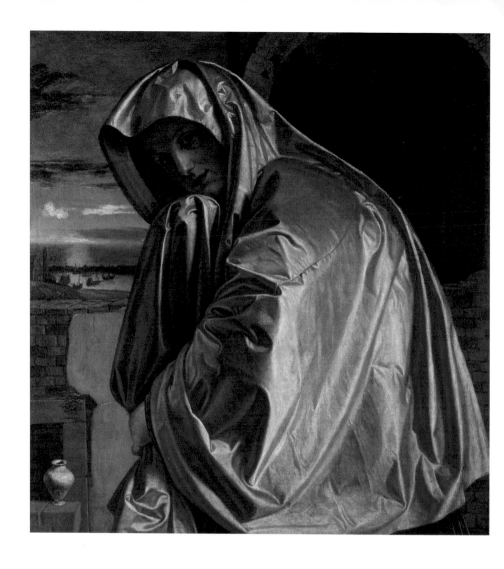

34. Giovanni Girolamo Savoldo,
Mary Magdalene, about 1535–40.
Savoldo worked predominantly
in Venice and the Veneto from
around 1520. Strongly influenced by
Giorgione, he seems mostly to have
painted figure groups (both religious
and secular) for wealthy collectors.

richly dressed, her golden hair loose, has eyes and tears only for her lord. Her face is, literally, an ancient mask of tragedy. The Virgin is one flesh with her Son, the mystical texts tell us: she experiences his sufferings, body and soul, and almost dies with him. Mary Magdalene's sorrow is different, more like the anguish of a woman who survives the death of her lover. In the imagery of Christ's death, she is the supreme heroine of earthly love and loss. But, as Neil MacGregor writes in his meditation on Titian's painting of the risen Christ appearing to the Magdalen [33], 'a lord who cannot be touched is a lord who can never be taken away'. Losing the man Jesus, whose body she can never again touch, Mary Magdalene finds God, and her own immortal soul.

Though representing a psychological and metaphysical drama of universal import, Titian depicts the Magdalen as a contemporary Venetian courtesan. In shock and deep mourning, she has come with her jar of precious ointment to anoint Jesus' body for the last time, yet she is dressed as if going out to dinner – the kind of party we know the artist enjoyed, with game, artichokes, beautiful women, wine and song. This is of course intended to evoke the occasion when, as a sinner, she anointed Jesus' feet with her hair, and to make the moment shown here even more poignant. But it is also intended, I cannot help but feel, to make the Magdalen, and thus the picture itself, more alluring to the viewer, particularly a male viewer. Some decades later, Savoldo, a Brescian artist who also worked in Venice, painted this very different image of Saint Mary Magdalene approaching the Sepulchre [34]. 'The first day of the week cometh Mary Magdalene early, when it was yet dark, unto the sepulchre...' (John 20:1). The picture is only slightly smaller than Titian's [33], but it is almost entirely filled with the figure of Mary. Savoldo focuses on her in 'close-up', precisely like a modern film director who wishes viewers to share a protagonist's feelings. Behind her we see the yawning darkness of Christ's sepulchre, displaced from the countryside near Jerusalem, perhaps to Venice's cemetery island of San Michele; in the distance the sun rises over the lagoon. More suitably dressed than Titian's Magdalen, Savoldo's figure is wrapped in a cloak – a cloak, however, of shimmering satin, whose virtuoso depiction is a hallmark of the painter's work. She has set down her jar of ointment by her side.

Savoldo may be picturing a specific moment in the Gospel text. Mary, having found the tomb empty, alerts Peter and the other disciples. After their return home, she remains alone by the sepulchre, weeping, convinced – even after speaking to two angels sitting in the tomb – that Jesus' body has been taken away and hidden.

35. Attributed to Correggio, *The Magdalen*, perhaps about 1518–19. Correggio was based in Parma during the High Renaissance, away from the major artistic centres of Florence, Rome and Venice. Nonetheless, his ethereal style exerted a profound influence on the development of Italian painting.

And when she had thus said, she turned herself back, and saw Jesus standing, and knew not that it was Jesus.

Jesus saith unto her, Woman, why weepest thou? whom seekest thou? She, supposing him to be the gardener, saith unto him, Sir, if thou have borne him hence, tell me where thou has laid him, and I will take him away. Jesus saith unto her, Mary. She turned herself, and saith unto him, Rabboni: which is to say, Master.
(John 20:11–17)

Mary 'turns herself' twice: first to speak to the gardener, then in recognition of her Master's voice. Her sorrow is tempered first by hope, then dispelled by tentative, half-disbelieving joy – and it is these transient expressions that, I believe, animate her face in Savoldo's painting. The spectator is meant to share in the drama of the revelation to Mary: Jesus Christ has truly risen from the dead. But in turning herself towards us, the Magdalen is, by definition, looking into the eyes of a male viewer. We see her from Christ's point of view. But there is another sense in which Savoldo's picture may have been designed to appeal to a male gaze – the gaze of someone not necessarily disposed to devotion or familiar with the Gospel text. When all is said and done, Savoldo shows a beautiful woman, luxuriously dressed, beckoning. Because images are so much more ambiguous than words, the painting allows itself to be read as a seductive invitation, possibly to an amorous encounter.

Images of the Magdalen living out the rest of her life in penitence in the wilderness of southern France, according to later legend, follow a similar pattern. As her fine clothes rotted away, it is said, her hair grew miraculously long to preserve her modesty. In a famous statue in Florence, the fifteenth-century sculptor Donatello showed her as an old woman, nearly toothless and scrawny from fasting, dressed only in abundant locks of hair. But, by the sixteenth century, collectors' pictures of the penitent Magdalen were less austere. A painting of about 1518, attributed to Correggio and known in several versions, makes the point [35]. In the bloom of youth, blond hair loose but not yet grown to cover her body, the saint artfully arranges what remains of her cloak to reveal her breasts and legs. She holds her attribute, the pot of ointment, and has a book propped up beside her, but she stares appealingly at the viewer with dark, lustrous eyes, a faint smile on her lips. Her pose and appearance disturbingly recall those of Venus, goddess of love and beauty, in Correggio's mythological picture, *Venus with Mercury and Cupid* [36].

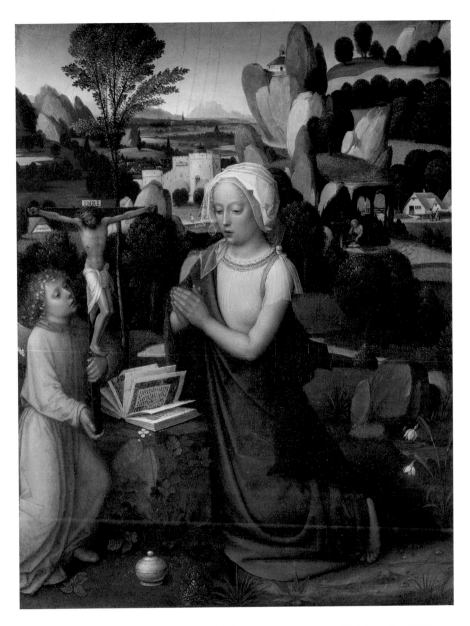

Opposite page: 36. Correggio,
Venus with Mercury and Cupid
('The School of Love'), about 1525.

Above: 37. Adriaen Ysenbrandt,
The Magdalen in a Landscape,
perhaps about 1510–25. Although
little of this artist's work remains
today, Ysenbrandt was a significant
painter in Bruges during the early
sixteenth century, becoming a
master in 1510.

Opposite page: 38. Master
of Liesborn, *The Annunciation*,
probably 1470–80. This unidentified
artist is known primarily for the
altarpiece at Liesborn Abbey,
in northern Germany, painted
in the mid-fifteenth century.

Right: Detail of *The Annunciation*.

The penitent Magdalen has another aspect, hinted at in
Correggio's picture but more fully developed in northern Europe
than in Italy, with its memories of pagan sculpture. She belongs
to that small elite of women who may be portrayed reading. Like
the scholarly Saint Jerome, she brings a bible with her into the
wilderness [37]. She also reads indoors. Rogier van der Weyden's
painting, made some time before 1438, is a fragment from an
altarpiece [39], but the image was soon adapted for private viewing
[40]. When the Virgin Mary is shown with a book, she is to be
understood as reading one of the Old Testament prophecies of her
role in the history of Salvation, such as Isaiah's: 'Behold, a virgin
shall conceive, and bear a son, and shall call his name Immanuel'
(Isaiah 7:14) [38]. Her reading symbolises her acquiescence to
God's plan. The Magdalen's reading is meant to be contemplative
and penitent. She has turned from the world to the Word of God.
But does this make fig. 37, and its many versions and variants,
suitable devotional pictures for women viewers?

Possibly. Yet there is to my eye something transgressive about
this image as well. The elegant youthful Magdalen, bejewelled and
dressed in the latest style, with red lips and downcast eyes, may
be demure, but she does not appear to be particularly penitent.
She owns a costly illuminated and lavishly bound manuscript.
In many households, her reading might have seemed a form of
ostentatious idleness, the ornament of one who neither toils nor
spins. She seems to me to represent yet another face of Woman,
as constructed in a male-dominated society ambivalent in its
feelings towards women.

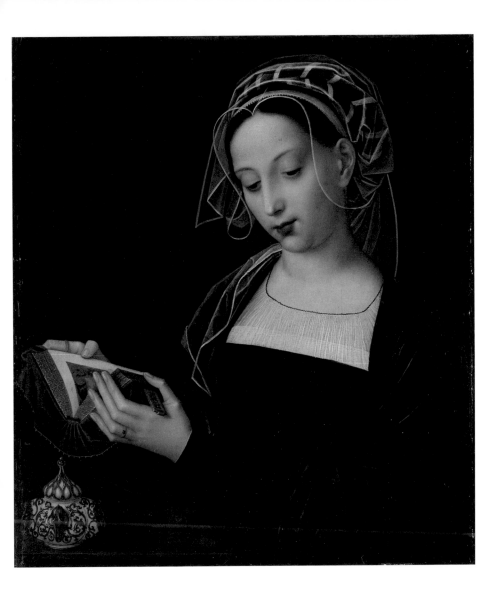

Opposite page: 39. Rogier van der
Weyden, *The Magdalen Reading*,
before 1438.

Above: 40. Ambrosius Benson,
The Magdalen Reading, about 1525.
Benson came from Lombardy, but
was active in Bruges, where he
became a master in the guild in
1519 and worked until his death.

PROTECTORS AND INTERCESSORS

Saints in Need, Saints Indeed

In addition to their role as intercessors, protectors and role models for communities, institutions, families and individuals, saints could be called upon by those in need of help. This remains perhaps their most familiar and popular function. Many people, even in Protestant or mainly secular countries, recall that Saint Jude – the apostle also known as Thaddeus or Lebbaeus – is the defender of last resort in lost causes, although we don't know why this should be so. According to the Golden Legend, he was martyred in Persia after performing many extraordinary miracles, and baptising 'more than sixty thousand people, not counting children'.

Other saints' legends clearly show why they have been invoked for particular afflictions. The principle is exactly

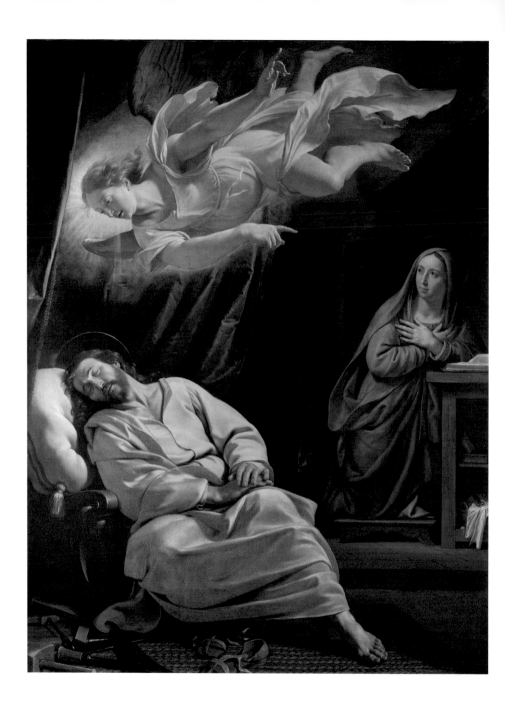

Opposite page: 41. Philippe de Champaigne, *The Dream of Saint Joseph*, 1642–3. Champaigne trained under Poussin, whose work exemplifed classicism in art. Champaigne became a founding member of the Acadèmie, a specialist state-sponsored art school in Paris, which encouraged high standards of artistic training and practice.

Right: 42. Pietro da Cortona, *Saint Cecilia*, 1620–5. Called after his native town of Cortona, Tuscany, Pietro moved to Rome in 1612. From 1633 to 1639 he executed one of the most influential decorative schemes in Rome, the Barberini Palace ceiling.

Previous pages: Detail of Annibale Carracci, *Christ appearing to Saint Anthony Abbot during his Temptation*, about 1598.

the same as when choosing saints to be the patrons of particular professions and trades: an affinity is found with the saints' way of life, or with the circumstances of their martyrdom. Cosmas and Damian, doctors, are patrons of physicians (and the Medici family) [11]; the apostle Luke, another doctor but also the only known Sunday-painter saint, is more often venerated by painters [12]. Jesus' foster-father, Joseph the carpenter (Matthew 13:55; Mark 6:3) naturally became the carpenters' patron saint, which is why Philippe de Champaigne spreads a modern assortment of wood-working tools at his feet in an altarpiece dedicated to him [41].

A more poetic tradition accounts for Saint Cecilia's patronage of music and musicians [42]. A real person of this name was buried in the early Christian Roman catacomb of San Callisto. The legendary Saint Cecilia, a beautiful girl of patrician rank, was betrothed to a young pagan, Valerian. On her wedding day she told him that she had consecrated her virginity to God, and persuaded him to be baptised, along with his brother. All three

43. Workshop of the Master of
the Saint Bartholomew Altarpiece,
*The Virgin and Child in Glory
with Saint James the Great and
Saint Cecilia*, about 1512, detail.
This anonymous German artist is
named after his Saint Bartholomew
Altarpiece which was made for the
church of St Columba, Cologne
(now Munich, Alte Pinakothek).
His work was influenced by
Netherlandish artists, notably
Rogier van der Weyden.

were put to death as obstinate Christians. A sixth-century hymn in her honour speaks of Cecilia singing to God 'in her heart' while musicians played at her wedding, and it is this touching particular with which she is forever associated. She is usually, as in fig. 42, represented with a portative organ. The anonymous German painter of a small domestic triptych altarpiece, probably made in Cologne around 1512, adds a further refinement [43]. On Saint Cecilia's right hand, gloved like that of a falconer, there perches a bird: nature's musician, singing God's praises as Cecilia did at her wedding, and as all human musicians ought at all times.

The same kind of association, often first made memorable through images, determined which saints to call on when in need. Even today, the dashboards of many cars, and the manly chests of many truck drivers, are decorated with medallions of Saint Christopher. He was the giant ferryman who, after his conversion by an elderly hermit, devoted his life to helping people cross a raging torrent, and once carried the infant Christ himself. His role as patron of travellers is made obvious in this sixteenth-century Netherlandish picture, where the torrent of legend becomes a sea dotted with ships [44]. Travelling remains a perilous business, and although not every medallion may testify to genuine faith, there remains the uneasy feeling that putting oneself under a saint's protection can do no harm. Even atheists, it used to be said, pray in the trenches.

Popular devotion like this is akin to sympathetic magic, that combats like with like. Another early Christian martyr, Saint Lucy, was said to have been loved by a pagan for the beauty of her eyes. Rather than give up her virginity, she plucked her eyes out to send to her rejected suitor (and was later denounced by him as a Christian, and put to death). Her somewhat gruesome attribute is a pair of eyes carried on a dish [45], and she has consequently been invoked for help by people with diseases of the eyes.

The hermit Saint Anthony Abbot was subject to temptations and tormented by demons who tore his flesh with their claws [46]. He became the patron of those afflicted with skin diseases, especially leprosy and ergotism. This painful, often fatal illness, that produced hallucinations as well as burning and itching, is caused by a fungus affecting rye, once the staple grain of northern Europe. Known as Saint Anthony's Fire, ergotism was rampant throughout Germany, the Netherlands and much of France. A religious order founded in Anthony's name was dedicated to its treatment, using, among their various therapies, balms and ointments derived from medicinal plants but made especially effective through contact with the saint's relics.

44. Style of the Master of the
Female Half-Lengths, *Saint
Christopher carrying the Infant
Christ*, about 1525–50, detail.
This work was once associated with
an unknown artist to which several
paintings have been ascribed. The
panel might have been produced
in Antwerp as it shows close
links with Flemish artists such as
Patenier and Ysenbrandt.

45. Carlo Crivelli, *Saint Lucy*,
about 1476, detail.

46. Annibale Carracci, *Christ
appearing to Saint Anthony Abbot
during his Temptation*, about 1598.

47. Giovanni di Paolo, *Saints Fabian and Sebastian*, about 1475. Giovanni di Paolo was one of the leading painters in Siena in the fifteenth century. His work is characterised by a typically decorative Sienese artistic style but with finely observed details from nature.

The greatest ill that threatened Europe, however, was bubonic plague, the dreaded Black Death: a bacterial disease that originated in Asia and, as we now know, was carried by the fleas of black rats. It first reached the West in 1348, killing between one-third and one-half of the population in a matter of months. Sporadic outbreaks continued to occur for many centuries; there were no effective remedies. Not surprisingly, especially since the cause of so great a disaster was thought to be the wrath of God, supernatural aid was sought.

Pagan Greeks and Romans had already drawn an analogy between the vindictive arrows of the gods and sores that afflicted the sick. So it was natural for Christians to invoke Saint Sebastian – martyred, though not killed, with arrows – against the plague, one of whose first symptoms was a swelling, or bubo, of the lymph nodes, which developed into festering wounds. Such invocations often added the promise, or vow, to thank the saint for his successful intercession. A late fifteenth-century Sienese painting may have been commissioned as just such a 'votive' thank offering by the brothers of the Misericordia, a charitable confraternity dedicated to the care and burial of plague victims [47]. Saint Sebastian, bristling with arrows, is accompanied by Saint Fabian, an early Christian pope and martyr who shares his feast-day. Two members of the brotherhood kneel at their feet, dressed and hooded in black and veiled against contagion.

At about the same time as this panel was painted in Siena, one of the most famous altarpieces of the Renaissance was completed by the Pollaiuolo brothers for the Oratory of Saint Sebastian in Florence, where the precious relic of the martyr's arm bone was kept [48]. Unlike their Sienese contemporary, the avant garde Florentines depicted the dramatic scene of the saint's martyrdom, the better to demonstrate their new-fangled mastery of anatomy, geometry, perspective, landscape, and ancient architecture. The altarpiece's single-panel rectangular format is an innovation, as is the use of oil paints. It is chastening for a present-day viewer to compare the Pollaiuolos' 'modern' masterpiece with Giovanni di Paolo's old-fashioned panel, and realise that they express fundamentally the same concerns and preoccupations, if not the same artistic ideals.

By this date, however, Saint Sebastian was often pictured in the company of another 'plague saint', Roch, Rock or Rocco – a fourteenth-century pilgrim who contracted the plague while nursing the sick during an epidemic in northern Italy. They appear together in innumerable altarpieces commissioned either during or after an epidemic. Many were found in cities, and

many others in specially built votive churches and chapels on the
pilgrimage and trade routes along which the plague also travelled.

In an early sixteenth-century example from near Ferrara [49],
Sebastian is raised in the centre, tied to a tall tree stump. Beneath
is a crossbow abandoned by the would-be executioners, and an
inconspicuous quartet of arrows pierce his flesh. On his right
stands Saint Roch, leaning on his pilgrim's staff, his bundle of
food and pilgrim's flask at his feet. His jerkin is asymmetrically
cut, the better to show off the bubo above his left knee. His
other traditional attribute, a companion dog, has been omitted,
perhaps because the artist or his clients felt the animal would have
been an indecorous presence above the altar. Balancing Roch on
Sebastian's left is a thoughtful Saint Demetrius, an early Christian
warrior saint and martyr, famous in the Eastern Church but so

S DEMET
RIVS

little known in the West that he is identified by a name tag. It is almost impossible, looking at this calm trio so strangely, yet so convincingly gathered together in a peaceful landscape, within sight of indifferent passers-by, to reconstruct the tormented circumstances in which this altarpiece, with its two plague saints, must have been commissioned. Suffering, death and the fear of death, and the grief, guilt and gratitude of survivors, are here sublimated into an image of serene trust and hope.

Real or legendary, the saints and martyrs assumed into Heaven remain among us on earth, in millions of images that show us whom to call upon for help when our own troubles are too great to bear – or too trivial to bother the Almighty with [50]. They mark out the feasts of the year, the years and seasons of our lives, our allegiances and duties. Though not to be worshipped as idols, they have inherited much of the appearance and nature of pagan divinities: some beautiful and alluring, others stern; some noble, others lowly. Like the ancient myths, the stories of their lives and deaths make exciting reading, yet it is mainly through images that they teach us what it means to believe; to sin and to repent; to suffer and rejoice; to endure or do battle; to live in solitude or in fellowship with others – or simply to enjoy images. They remind us of who we are, and what we can become, of the limits and potentials of our own nature. We can, as we wish, view them as projections of our own human needs, or as evidence of the grace of God.

50. Fra Angelico, *The Virgin Mary with the Apostles and Other Saints*, about 1423–4. Born Guido di Pietro, this painter lived in a Dominican friary in Florence, where he painted his greatest works for the friars and their Medici sponsors. Summoned to Rome in 1445, he was active there and in Orvieto before returning to Florence.

FIND OUT MORE

The main source of information about earlier saints is *The Golden Legend*, available in various editions, including:

Jacobus de Voragine, *The Golden Legend: Reading on the Saints*, Princeton 1995

Jacobus de Voragine, *The Golden Legend* (selections), London 2006

For further information about saints in National Gallery paintings, see:

D. Bomford, J. Dunkerton, D. Gordon, A. Roy and J. Kirby, *Art in the Making: Italian Painting before 1400*, London 2000

J. Dunkerton, S. Foister, D. Gordon and N. Penny, *Giotto to Dürer: Early Renaissance Painting in the National Gallery*, London and New Haven 1991

General:

D. Attwater and C. John, *The Penguin Dictionary of Saints*, London 2005

F. L. Cross and E. A. Livingstone, *The Oxford Dictionary of the Christian Church*, Oxford 2005

G. Duchet-Suchaux and M. Pastoureau, *The Bible and the Saints*, Paris 1994

D. H. Farmer, *The Oxford Dictionary of Saints*, Oxford 2004

L. Govier, *The National Gallery Visitor's Guide*, London 2009
This book contains a self-guided tour, 'Life of Christ', providing insight into a number of paintings in the National Gallery Collection depicting saints.

SPOTTING SAINTS

Some saints you're likely to see in the National Gallery

Saint Ambrose (of Milan)
Attributes: garbed as a bishop (in episcopal vestments, carrying a mitre and T-shaped crozier) or by a beehive
Patron saint of: bee keepers, candlemakers and Milan

Saint Anne
Attributes: her daughter, Virgin Mary, and Christ, or with a book teaching young Mary to read
Patron saint of: childbirth, mothers and republican Florence

Saint Barbara
Attributes: a tower, which her pagan father kept her locked up in to keep her from the outside world
Patron saint of: prisoners and against fire and lightning

Saint Benedict
Attributes: sometimes shown with a broken cup and a serpent
Patron saint of: monks, and protection against poison

Saint Bernardino of Siena
Attributes: a tablet or bible inscribed with IHS, Jesus' name in the form of Greek monogram
Patron saint of: public relations

Saint Catherine of Alexandria
Attributes: a wheel, on which she was martyred
Patron saint of: philosophers, preachers and students

Saint Christopher
Attributes: holding a tree branch for support and crossing a river, often carrying the Christ Child
Patron saint of: travel

Saint Dominic
Attributes: a black cloak and hood over a white tunic, and sometimes symbolised as a dog
Patron saint of: astronomy and the falsely accused

Saint Dorothy
Attributes: a basket of fruit and flowers
Patron saint of: brides, newly weds and florists

Saint Eustace
Attributes: often shown with a stag, of which he is said to have seen Jesus' face between the antlers
Patron saint of: hunters and those facing adversity

Saint Francis of Assisi
Attributes: wearing a modest brown habit and a belt with three knots, representing the three vows of poverty, chastity and obedience
Patron saint of: animals, peace and Italy

Saint Gabriel Archangel
Attrbutes: holding a lily, a sign of purity
Patron saint of: messengers and communication

Saint George
Attributes: wearing armour and slaying a dragon that is holding a maiden captive
Patron saint of: horsemen, soldiers and England

Saint Jerome
Attributes: either shown in his study with books or in rags with a lion – legend has it that he pulled a thorn from the foot of a beast
Patron saint of: libraries, librarians and scholars

Saint John the Baptist
Attributes: a lamb, dressed in camel skins, or with a staff
Patron saint of: Baptism – he baptized Christ

Saint John the Evangelist
Attributes: an eagle, sometimes with a pen or inkhorn in its mouth; represents far-sightedness
Patron saint of: brotherly love and affection

Saint Joseph
Attributes: a square or tools, a staff or the infant Jesus
Patron saint of: the Universal Church and workers

Saint Lawrence
Attributes: a martyr's palm and a grid iron are symbols of his martyrdom – he was grilled to death
Patron saint of: the poor, the neglected, tanners and cooks

Saint Lucy
Attributes: carrying a pair of eyes on a dish
Patron saint of: the blind

Saint Luke
Attributes: often presented with a bull or painting the Madonna and Child
Patron saint of: artists and physicians

Saint Margaret of Antioch
Attributes: depicted with a slain dragon
Patron saint of: pregnancy

Saint Martin of Tours
Attributes: shown cutting his cloak in two, to give half to a ragged beggar, or with a beggar standing nearby
Patron saint of: poverty

Saint Mary Magdalene
Attributes: a container of ointment, often grieving at the foot of the cross
Patron saint of: sinners

Saint Matthew
Attributes: often depicted as a tax collector
Patron saint of: accountants, bankers and tax collectors

Saint Paul
Attributes: a sword or having fallen from a horse
Patron saint of: the City of London

Saint Peter
Attributes: holding two crossed keys to Heaven; representing the powers of absolution and excommunication
Patron saint of: righteousness, the Papacy and Rome

Saint Roch
Attributes: a thigh wound and a dog offering bread
Patron saint of: invalids and against pestilence

Saint Sebastian
Attributes: shown tied to a post and shot with arrows; the depiction of his arrow-wounds became synonymous with the plague
Patron saint of: athletes and the plague

Saint Stephen
Attributes: three stones and the martyr's palm – he was martyred by being stoned to death
Patron saint of: stonemasons and headaches

Saint Thomas
Attributes: seen placing his finger in the side of Christ, hence being known as 'doubting Thomas', or shown with an architect's square
Patron saint of: architects

Saint Veronica
Attributes: a cloth depicting Jesus' face referencing the tale where she wiped Jesus' face while he was carrying the cross, and an image of his features miraculously appeared on the cloth
Patron saint of: laundry workers

ENJOY MORE NATIONAL GALLERY BOOKS

Colour

David Bomford and
Ashok Roy

This book uncovers the ways
in which artists have used
colour, and describes the
pigments characteristic of a
particular period, the effect
on colour of the painter's
chosen medium, and how the
development of new pigments
dramatically extended
the palette.

Conservation of Paintings

David Bomford; updated by Jill
Dunkerton and Martin Wyld

Explores the material nature
of paintings, outlining how
they fare with age and the
main types of conservation
technique carried out on
canvases and panels. With
new case studies, this book
delves into the complex and
varied issues surrounding the
conservation of paintings.

Faces

Alexander Sturgis

The artist's portrayal of the face
often communicates drama,
character and narrative within
an artwork. This guide, updated
with new comparisons, leads
the reader through a lively
and fresh account of facial
stereotypes, pose, technical
conventions and catching
a likeness.

FSC

Mixed Sources

Product group from well-managed
forests and other controlled sources

Cert no. SGS-COC-002987
www.fsc.org
© 1996 Forest Stewardship Council

National Gallery publications generate valuable revenue for
the Gallery, to ensure that future generations are able to enjoy
the paintings as we do today. See www.nationalgallery.org.uk.
For our latest titles and special offers, visit our online shop
www.nationalgallery.co.uk/shop. All works © The National
Gallery, London 2009.